Published By Nicholas Thompson

How to Start the Pegan Diet: Tips and

Tricks

ISBN 978-87-94477-46-8

TABLE OF CONTENTS

PAN-SEARED SALMON WITH KALE AND APPLE SALAD

Ingredients:

- Kosher salt

- 1 bunch kale, ribs removed, leaves very thinly sliced (about 6 cups)

- ¼ cup dates

- 1 H2ycrisp apple

- ¼ cup finely grated pecorino

- 3 Tbsp toasted slivered almonds

- Freshly ground black pepper

- 4 5-oz center- cut salmon fillets (about 1" thick)

- 3 Tbsp fresh lemon juice

- 3 Tbsp olive oil

- 4 whole wheat dinner rolls

Directions:

1. Bring the salmon to room temperature 10 minutes before cooking.

2. Meanwhile, whisk together the lemon juice, 2 tablespoons of the olive oil and 1/4 teaspoon salt in a large bowl. Add the kale, toss to coat and let stand 10 minutes.

3. While the kale stands, cut the dates into thin slivers and the apple into matchsticks. Add the dates, apples, cheese and almonds to the kale. Season with pepper, toss well and set aside.

4. Sprinkle the salmon all over with 1/2 teaspoon salt and some pepper. Heat the remaining 1 tablespoon oil in a large nonstick skillet over medium-low heat. Raise the heat to medium-high.

5. Place the salmon, skin-side up in the pan. Cook until golden brown on 2 side, about 4 minutes.

6. Turn the fish over with a spatula, and cook until it feels firm to the touch, about 3 minutes more.

7. Divide the salmon, salad and rolls evenly among four plates.

VEGETABLE VEGAN FRITTATA

Ingredients:

- 1 zucchini, diced

- 2 cloves garlic, minced

- Handful grape tomatoes, halved or quartered

- Pinch of red pepper flakes, optional

- Mineral salt and pepper, to taste

- 1 tablespoon olive oil or ¼ cup water (for water saute)

- 2 medium potatoes, diced (with or without the skin)

- 1 small onion, diced

- 1 bell pepper, diced

For the blender/food processor:

- 1 ½ teaspoons dried tarragon, thyme or basil (or a combo)

- ½ teaspoon garlic powder

- ½ teaspoon salt

- ¼ teaspoon turmeric

- ⅛ teaspoon pepper (black or white)

- 1 package (16 oz) organic silken tofu (soft or firm), drained (no pressing needed)

- ¼ cup unsweetened non-dairy milk

- 2 heaping teaspoons cornstarch, arrowroot or tapioca flour

- 2 – 3 tablespoons nutritional yeast

- 1 teaspoon mustard (any kind) or ½ teaspoon mustard powder

Directions:

1. Preheat oven to 375 degrees F.

2. Saute: Heat oil in a pan over medium heat, saute potatoes for 5 minutes, add onion and cook an additional 5 minutes.

3. Add bell pepper, zucchini and garlic, cook until softened. Add tomatoes and optional red pepper flakes, cook another minute or two. Season with salt and pepper to taste.

4. Tofu egg: In a food processor/blender, combine the remaining Ingredients: and process until smooth. Then taste for seasoning.

5. Assemble: Add the tofu mixture to the pan the vegetables cooked in and mix well. Spoon mixture into a lightly greased 9 inch round pie/quiche dish or springform pan. Level the top flat with the back of a spatula or spoon and make sure all edges are filled.

6. Bake: Place on the middle rack and bake for 35 – 45 minutes, frittata should be firm to the

touch. If top starts to brown too much, cover with foil or small silpat.

7. Remove and let cool for at least 10 minutes. If using a pie/quiche dish, loosen the edges of the frittata, place a plate over top and carefully flip so frittata falls onto the plate and serve (this step is optional).

8. This frittata is wonderful with sliced avocado and a little sriracha for heat.

9. Store: Leftovers can be stored in the refrigerator for 4 – 5 days. To keep longer, store in the freezer using freezer safe containers for up to 2 – 3 months.

BLUEBERRY AND CHIA SMOOTHIE

Ingredients:

- 2 cups unsweetened nondairy milk

- 2 cups blueberries, fresh or frozen

- 2 tablespoons pure maple syrup or agave

- 2 tablespoons chia seeds

- 2 tablespoons cocoa powder

Directions:

1. Blend together the soaked chia seeds, almond milk, blueberries, maple syrup, and cocoa powder and blend until smooth. Serve immediately

APPLE AND CINNAMON OATMEAL

Ingredients:

- 2/3 cup rolled oats

- 1 teaspoon ground cinnamon

- 1/4 cups apple cider

- 1 apple, peeled, cored, and chopped

- 1 tablespoon pure maple syrup

Directions:

2. Take the apple cider to a boil over medium-high heat. Stir in the apple, oats, and cinnamon.

3. Bring the cereal to a boil and turn down the heat to low.

4. Simmer until the oatmeal thickens, 3 to 4 minutes. Spoon into 3 bowls and sweeten with maple syrup if using. Serve hot.

NUT PACKED MORNING PORRIDGE

Ingredients:

- 1 cup pecan, halved

- 2 tablespoons stevia

- 4 teaspoons coconut oil, melted

- 1 cup cashew nuts, raw and unsalted

- 2 cups of water

Directions:

1. Chop the nuts in a food processor and form a smooth paste
2. Add water, oil, stevia to nuts paste and transfer the mix to a saucepan
3. Stir cook for 5 minutes on high heat
4. Lower heat to low and simmer for 10 minutes
5. Serve warm and enjoy!

THE SMOOTH GREEN SMOOTHIE

Ingredients:

- 1 tablespoon coconut flakes, unsweetened

- 1 cup of water

- 2 cups spring mix salad

- 1 cup whole milk

- 1 pack stevia

- 1 tablespoon coconut oil

Directions:

1. Add listed Ingredients: to a blender

2. Blend until you have a smooth and creamy texture

3. Serve chilled and enjoy!

BASIL & PARMESAN STEAKS

Ingredients:

- ½ tablespoon pine nuts

- ½ cup diced mushrooms

- ½ tablespoons diced parsley

- ½ tablespoon olive oil

- 2 cups of lean strips of steaks

- ½ tablespoon diced oregano

Directions:

1. In a hot skillet cook steak strips over olive oil approx. 1 minute and transfer to plates.

2. Sauté pine nuts and mushroom 30-45 seconds and spoon over steak strips before topping with parsley and oregano.

BELL PEPPER AND RICE SOUP

Ingredients:

- 1 red bell pepper, julienned

- ½ Tbsp diced thyme

- 1/3 teaspoon black pepper

- 3 cups organic vegetable broth

- ½ cup basmati rice

- 2 oz leftover ground beef or hamburger crumble (optional)

Directions:

1. In a pot bring broth, rice kernels, julienned bell pepper, thyme, pepper, and ground beef to a boil.

2. Reduce heat, cover, and let simmer 15-20 minutes.

3. With hamburger-

AVOCADO EGGS

Ingredients:

- Chive

- Epaulette pepper

- Salt

- Eggs: 4

- Lawyers: 2

- Pepper

Directions:

1. Preheat the oven to 220 ° C.

2. Cut the avocados in half. Remove some of the avocado flesh with a spoon so you can place an egg on it.

3. Place the avocado halves in a tight baking pan, tight against each other.

4. Crack 1 egg into each avocado half; season
    with salt, pepper and Epaulette pepper.

5. Bake for 15 to 20 minutes. Serve sprinkled
    with chopped chives.

BUCKWHEAT PORRIDGE

Ingredients:

- 1 cinnamon stick

- 1 teaspoon alcohol-and gluten-free pure vanilla extract generous pinch of sea salt

- 4 tablespoons maple syrup 150 g mixed berries

- 165 g buckwheat groats

- 750 ml unsweetened Almond Milk

- 2 tablespoons unsweetened shredded coconut, toasted

Directions:

1. Put the buckwheat groats in a saucepan and add the almond milk, cinnamon, vanilla and salt.

2. Cover and cook over a medium heat, stirring occasionally, until the buckwheat is tender and has absorbed the milk, about 20 minutes. Discard the cinnamon stick.

3. Divide the porridge between 4 bowls.

4. Drizzle each portion with 1 tablespoon of the maple syrup, top equally with the berries, and sprinkle with the toasted coconut. Serve.

CHAI PANCAKES

Ingredients:

For Pancakes:

- 1 tsp baking powder

- ¼ cup raw pecans, crushed

- ½ tsp nutmeg, ground

- 2 tsp cinnamon, ground

- ½ tsp cloves, ground

- ½ tsp baking soda

- ¼ tsp cardamom, ground

- ¼ tsp salt

- ¼ tsp ginger, ground

- 1 ½ cups almond milk, unsweetened

- 2 large eggs

- 1 cup buckwheat flour

- ½ cup almond flour

- 2 tsp pure vanilla extract

- ¼ cup coconut oil, melted

- 3 tbsp granulated monk fruit sweetener (optional)

- Maple syrup, for topping (optional)

For Coconut Whipped Cream:

- ⅓ cup powdered monk fruit

- 14-oz can of coconut cream, chilled overnight

Directions:

For Pancakes:

1. If making the whipping cream, refrigerate a large mixing bowl.

2. In a second large bowl for the pancake mixture.

3. Beat the granulated monk fruit sweetener (optional), 2 tablespoons of coconut oil, almond milk, eggs, and vanilla extract until the mixture is fluffy.

4. Gently fold in the crushed pecans.

5. Get a third large bowl and sift 1 ½ teaspoons cinnamon, ginger, nutmeg, cardamom, cloves, baking soda, baking powder, salt, buckwheat, and almond flour.

6. Spoon the dry Ingredients: slowly into the wet mixture and stir until no more lumps remain.

7. Heat a skillet over medium heat and when hot add about a teaspoon of the remaining coconut oil.

8. Cover the surface of the skillet with the oil before adding 2–3 ¼ cups of the batter to it. This can depend on the size of the skillet you are using.

9. Cook each side of the pancake for 3 minutes or until golden brown.

10. Add the pancake to a fresh plate and continue to add coconut oil and butter until no batter remains.

For Whipped Cream:

11. Remove the chilled canned coconut cream and mixing bowl from the fridge.

12. Add the solid cream portion from the can and add it to the bowl.

13. Use a hand mixer to mix the cream, ½ teaspoon of cinnamon, and the powdered monk fruit for about 3 minutes. The mixture should be smooth.

14. Serve the pancakes topped with the cream, a drizzle of maple syrup, and whatever fresh fruit you so desire.

PEGAN-FRIENDLY GRANOLA

Ingredients:

- ½ cup walnuts, chopped

- 3 tbsp coconut oil, melted

- 1 cup toasted coconut chips or pieces, unsweetened

- 2 tsp cinnamon, ground

- ¼ cup cacao nibs

- ½ cup raisins

- ½ cup sunflower seeds, unsalted

- ½ cup hazelnuts, chopped

- 1–2 tbsp maple syrup, depending on your sweet tooth

Directions:

1. Preheat the oven to 350 °F.

2. Get a large rimmed baking sheet and line it with some parchment paper.

3. Add the nuts and seeds to the baking sheet and sprinkle them with coconut oil, cinnamon, and maple syrup.

4. Mix well and ensure everything is coated.

5. Bake mixture for 5–7 minutes and watch closely to not let the mixture burn.

6. Remove from the oven and mix in the cacao nibs, coconut chips, and raisins.

7. Can be enjoyed immediately with some fresh fruit and some dairy-free milk or eaten once cooled.

8. When storing the granola, ensure that it is completely cooled before placing it in an airtight container. It can last for up to 2 month.

PORTOBELLO MUSHROOM BURGER

Ingredients:

- 2 tablespoons balsamic vinegar

- 2 tablespoons olive oil

- 2 lettuce leaves

- 2 tomato slices

- 2 red onion slices

- 2 large Portobello mushrooms

- 2 whole wheat burger buns

- Salt and pepper to taste

Directions:

1. Preheat the grill or grill pan to medium-high heat.

2. Mix balsamic vinegar, olive oil, salt, and pepper in a small bowl.

3. Brush the Portobello mushrooms with the mixture.

4. Grill the mushrooms for 4-5 minutes on each
   side.

5. Toast the burger buns lightly.

6. Assemble the burger by placing a mushroom
   on each bun, followed by lettuce, tomato, and
   red onion. Serve and enjoy!

CAULIFLOWER FRIED RICE

Ingredients:

- 1 cup mixed vegetables (carrots, peas, corn)

- 2 garlic cloves, minced

- 2 tablespoons tamari sauce

- 2 green onions, chopped

- 2 cups cauliflower rice

- 1 tablespoon coconut oil

- Salt and pepper to taste

Directions:

1. In a large skillet over medium heat, melt the coconut oil.

2. Add minced garlic and sauté until fragrant.

3. Add mixed vegetables and cook until tender.

4. Stir in cauliflower rice and tamari sauce, cooking for 5 minutes.

5. Season with salt and pepper.

6. Garnish with chopped green onions before serving.

QUINOA AND LENTIL STUFFED PEPPERS

Ingredients:

- Four large bell peppers (any colour)

- 1 cup cooked quinoa

- 1 cup cooked lentils

- 2 small onion, finely chopped

- 3 cloves garlic, minced

- 2 carrot, grated

- 2 celery stalk, finely chopped

- 1 cup diced tomatoes

- 2 teaspoon of dried oregano

- 2 teaspoon of dried basil

- 1/2 teaspoon cumin

- Salt and pepper to taste

- 1/2 cup shredded mozzarella cheese (optional)

- Fresh parsley, chopped (for garnish)

Directions:

1. Preheat the oven to 375°F (190°C).
2. Cut off the tops of the bell peppers and remove the seeds and membranes. Rinse them well.
3. In a large mixing bowl, combine the cooked quinoa, lentils, onion, garlic, carrot, celery, diced tomatoes, dried oregano, dried basil, cumin, salt, and pepper. Mix well to combine.
4. Stuff each bell pepper with the quinoa and lentil mixture, packing it tightly. Place the stuffed peppers upright in a baking dish.
5. If desired, sprinkle shredded mozzarella cheese over each stuffed pepper.

6. Cover the baking dish with foil and bake in the oven for 30 minutes.

7. Remove the foil and bake for an additional 10-15 minutes, or until the peppers are tender and the cheese is melted and bubbly.

8. Remove from the oven and let the stuffed peppers cool for a few minutes. Garnish with fresh chopped parsley before serving.

SPAGHETTI SQUASH PAD THAI

Ingredients:

- 3 tablespoons of vegetable oil

- 2 small onion, finely chopped

- 2 cloves garlic, minced

- 1 red bell pepper, thinly sliced

- 2 carrot, julienned

- 1 cup bean sprouts

- 2 green onions, chopped

- 1/4 cup roasted peanuts, chopped (optional)

- Fresh cilantro leaves for garnish

- 2 medium-sized spaghetti squash

For the Pad Thai Sauce:

- 3 tablespoons brown sugar

- 2 tablespoon fish sauce (optional for non-vegetarian version)

- 2 teaspoon sriracha sauce (adjust to taste)

- 4 tablespoons soy sauce

- 3 tablespoons of lime juice

- 3 tablespoons tamarind paste

Directions:

1. Preheat your oven to 400°F (200°C). Cut the spaghetti squash in half lengthwise and scoop out the seeds.

2. Place the squash halves on a baking sheet, cut side up. Bake in the preheated oven for 25-30 minutes or until the squash is tender. Once cooked, remove it from the oven and let it cool for a few minutes.

3. While the squash is cooking, prepare the Pad
    Thai sauce. In a small bowl, whisk together
    the soy sauce, lime juice, tamarind paste,
    brown sugar, fish sauce (if using), and sriracha
    sauce. Set aside.

4. Heat the vegetable oil in a large skillet or wok
    over medium-high heat. Add the onion and
    garlic, and sauté for 2-3 minutes until fragrant
    and translucent.

5. Add the red bell pepper, carrot, and bean
    sprouts to the skillet. Stir-fry for another 3-4
    minutes until the vegetables are tender-crisp.

6. Using a fork, scrape the flesh of the cooked
    spaghetti squash into the skillet with the
    vegetables. Toss everything together until
    well combined.

7. Pour the Pad Thai sauce over the mixture in
    the skillet. Stir-fry for an additional 2-3
    minutes to allow the flavors to meld together.

8. Remove the skillet from the heat and garnish
    with chopped green onions and roasted
    peanuts (if using). Serve the Spaghetti Squash
    Pad Thai hot, garnished with fresh cilantro
    leaves.

SPINACH AND FETA STUFFED PORTOBELLO MUSHROOMS

Ingredients:

- 1 small onion diced

- 2 cloves of garlic minced

- 3 cups of spinach leave

- 1/4 cup of crumbled feta cheese

- 4 Portobello mushrooms

- 1 tbsp olive oil

- Salt

- Pepper

Directions:

1. Preheat the oven to 375 F. Remove the stems
    of the Portobello mushrooms and gently
    scrape out the gills.

2. Brush both sides of the mushrooms with olive
    oil and season with salt and pepper. In a
    skillet over medium heat, sauté the onion and
    garlic until softened.

3. Add the spinach and cook until wilted. Mix in
    the feta cheese and spoon the mixture into
    the mushroom caps.

4. Place the mushrooms on a baking sheet and
    bake for 15-20 minutes, or until the
    mushrooms are tender.

BANANA NUT BISCUITS

Ingredients:

- 1/4 cup coconut oil, melted

- 1/2 cup almond flour

- 1/4 cup coconut flour

- 1 teaspoon baking powder

- 1/2 teaspoon cinnamon

- 2 ripe bananas, mashed

- 3 large eggs

- 1/4 cup almond butter

- 1/4 cup chopped walnuts

Directions:

1. Preheat your stove to 350°F (175°C) and line a biscuit tin with paper liners.

2. Mix the mashed bananas, eggs, almond butter, and melted coconut oil in a large mixing bowl until well combined.

3. In a different bowl, combine as 2 the almond flour, coconut flour, baking powder, and cinnamon.

4. Continuously add the dry fixings to the wet fixings, mixing until you have a smooth player.

5. Add the chopped walnuts by hand.

6. Partition the hitter equally among the biscuit cups.

7. Prepare for 20-25 minutes or until a toothpick embedded into the focal point of a biscuit tells the truth.

8. Permit the biscuits to cool in the tin for a couple of moments prior to moving them to a wire rack to totally cool.

VEGGIE BREAKFAST SKILLET

Ingredients:

- 1/2 red bell pepper, chopped

- 1/2 yellow bell pepper, chopped

- 1/2 zucchini, sliced

- 1 cup baby spinach

- 4 large eggs

- 2 tablespoons coconut oil

- 1 small sweet potato, diced

- Salt and pepper to taste

- Fresh chopped parsley for garnish

Directions:

1. In a large skillet, heat coconut oil to a medium temperature.

2. Add the diced yam and cook for around 5
    minutes until marginally mellowed.
3. Add the cleaved ringer peppers and zucchini
    to the skillet and cook for another 3-4 minutes
    until the vegetables are delicate.
4. Cook until the baby spinach is wilted by
    stirring in.
5. Make four wells in the vegetables and break
    an egg into each well.
6. Cook the eggs to your ideal degree of d2ness,
    covering the skillet with a top for a couple of
    moments on the off chance that you favor the
    eggs to be completely cooked.
7. Season with salt and pepper to taste and
    embellishment with new slashed parsley prior
    to serving.

SPINACH ON TOMATO PLATES

Ingredients:

- 4 tomatoes

- 20 c. chopped mature spinach

- ½ tsp. salt

- Olive oil

- ½ tsp. black pepper

- 1 chopped medium onion

Directions:

1. In a skillet, heat 3 tablespoons of olive oil and add onion to sauté for one minute.

2. Add spinach and seasonings to sauté until wilted.

3. Top each tomato with spinach with tomato slices.

4. Serve and enjoy!

CARROT CAKE SMOOTHIE

Ingredients:

- 1 tbsp. fresh grated ginger

- ½ c. coconut milk

- ½ tsp. nutmeg

- ½ c. ice

- 3 tbsps. honey

- ½ tsp. cinnamon

- 2 steamed and cooled carrots

Directions:

1. Put all the Ingredients:in a blender and mix until smooth.

2. Serve and enjoy

MEXICAN ROASTED CAULIFLOWER

Ingredients:

- 1/2 tsp onion powder

- 1/4 tsp cumin

- 3/4 tsp salt

- 1/4 tsp black pepper

- 1/4 cup cilantro

- 1/4 cup green or red onion diced

- 3 fresh lime wedges

- 1 large head cauliflower, cut into florets

- 2 tbsp avocado oil

- 1 tsp chili powder

- 1/2 tsp garlic powder

- 1/2 avocado sliced

Directions:

1. Preheat oven to 425 degrees F

2. Toss cauliflower florets with avocado oil, chili powder, garlic powder, onion powder, cumin, salt, and pepper. Make sure the spices are well-distributed..

3. Spread evenly on a baking sheet lined with parchment paper and roast for about 20 minutes.

4. Remove from the oven and flip cauliflower for even cooking. Roast an additional 10-12 minutes, until tender with crispy edges.

5. Remove from the oven and serve topped with fresh cilantro, onion, lime wedges and avocado.

STRAWBERRY COCONUT SMOOTHIE

Ingredients:

- 1 c. banana frozen and sliced

- 2 c. strawberries frozen

- 1 tsp. vanilla extract

- 1 c. coconut milk

- 1 scoop vegan friendly protein powder optional

Directions:

1. Begin by placing all Ingredients: into your blender and blending until smooth.

2. You can add additional coconut milk to reach desired consistency. Serve and enjoy!

TUNA SALAD

Ingredients:

- 1/4 cup diced bell peppers (any color)

- 2 tablespoons chopped fresh parsley

- 2 tablespoons chopped fresh dill

- 2 tablespoons capers, rinsed and drained
  Juice of 1 lemon

- 2 tablespoons extra virgin olive oil Salt and pepper to taste

- 2 cans of sustainably sourced tuna (packed in water or olive oil), drained

- 1/4 cup diced red onion

- 1/4 cup diced celery

- 1/4 cup diced cucumber

- Lettuce leaves or mixed greens, for serving

  Sliced avocado, for garnish (optional)

Directions:

1. In a large mixing bowl, combine the drained tuna, diced red onion, celery, cucumber, bell peppers, parsley, dill, and capers.
2. In a separate small bowl, whisk together the lemon juice, extra virgin olive oil, salt, and pepper.
3. Pour the dressing over the tuna combination and lightly toss to coat all the substances evenly.
4. Taste and adjust the seasoning if needed. Allow the salad to marinate in the refrigerator for at least 15 minutes to allow the flavors to meld together.
5. When ready to serve, line a plate or bowl with lettuce leaves or mixed greens.
6. Spoon the Pegan Tuna Salad onto the bed of lettuce.

7. Garnish with sliced avocado, if desired, for an
    extra creamy and nutritious touch.

8. Serve the Pegan Tuna Salad as a refreshing
    and protein-packed main dish or enjoy it as a
    filling for lettuce wraps, stuffed inside a pita
    pocket, or atop whole-grain bread.

9. The Pegan Tuna Salad is a versatile and
    satisfying option for lunch or a light dinner. It
    offers a balance of protein from the tuna,
    along with a medley of fresh vegetables and
    herbs that provide an array of nutrients.

10. Remember to choose sustainably sourced
    tuna for both your health and the
    environment. Enjoy this flavorful and
    nourishing Pegan twist on the classic tuna
    salad!

CAULIFLOWER FRIED RICE

Ingredients:

- 2 cloves of garlic, minced

- 1 small onion, finely chopped

- 1 cup mixed vegetables (carrots, peas, corn, bell peppers, etc.)

- 2 eggs, beaten

- 2 tablespoons soy sauce or tamari sauce (gluten-free option)

- 1 tablespoon oyster sauce (optional)

- 1\/2 teaspoon ground ginger

- 1 medium-sized cauliflower head

- 2 tablespoons vegetable oil or sesame oil

- Salt and pepper to taste

- Green onions, chopped (for garnish)

Directions:

1. Cut the cauliflower into florets and discard the stems. Place the florets in a food processor and pulse until they resemble rice-like grains. You can also use a grater to achieve a similar texture.

2. Heat the vegetable oil or sesame oil in a large skillet or wok over medium heat.

3. Add the minced garlic and chopped onion to the pan and sauté for about 2 minutes until they become fragrant and slightly softened.

4. Add the mixed vegetables to the pan and cook for an additional 3-4 minutes, or until they are tender-crisp.

5. Push the vegetables to 2 side of the pan and pour the beaten eggs into the other side.

6. Scramble the eggs until they are fully cooked, breaking them into small pieces.

7. Incorporate the cauliflower rice into the pan and stir-fry everything together, combining the vegetables, eggs, and cauliflower.

8. Add the soy sauce or tamari sauce, oyster sauce (if using), ground ginger, salt, and pepper to the pan. Stir-fry for another 2-3 minutes until everything is well coated and heated through.

9. Taste and modify the seasoning if needed. Remove the cauliflower fried rice from the heat and garnish with chopped green onions.

10. Serve the cauliflower fried rice as a flavorful and nutritious main dish or as a side dish alongside your favorite protein.

11. Cauliflower fried rice is a versatile dish, and you can customize it by adding other Ingredients: such as diced chicken, shrimp, or tofu for added protein. It's a great option for those following a low-carb, gluten-free, or

keto diet. Enjoy this healthier twist on a classic favorite!

COCONUT FLOUR PANCAKES WITH WILD BLUEBERRIES

Ingredients:

- 1/4 teaspoon ground cinnamon

- 4 eggs

- 1/4 cup unsweetened almond milk

- 2 tablespoons h2y

- 1 teaspoon vanilla extract

- 1/2 cup fresh or frozen wild blueberries

- 1/2 cup coconut flour

- 1/2 teaspoon baking powder

- 1/4 teaspoon salt

- Coconut oil or butter for cooking

Directions:

1. In a medium bowl, whisk together the coconut flour, baking powder, salt, and cinnamon.
2. In another bowl, beat the eggs, almond milk, h2y, and vanilla extract together until well combined.
3. Add the dry Ingredients: to the wet Ingredients: and mix until a thick batter forms.
4. Gently fold in the blueberries.
5. Heat a non-stick pan or griddle over medium heat and melt a little coconut oil or butter in it.
6. Using a 1/4 cup measuring cup, scoop the batter onto the pan, spreading it slightly with the back of the scoop.
7. Cook until bubbles form on the surface, then flip and cook until golden brown on both sides.
8. Repeat with the remaining batter, adding more coconut oil or butter to the pan as

needed.

BREAKFAST HASH WITH SWEET POTATO AND BRUSSELS SPROUTS

Ingredients:

- 4 cloves garlic, minced

- 4 tablespoons olive oil

- 1 teaspoon smoked paprika

- Salt and pepper, to taste

- 2 medium sweet potatoes, peeled and diced into small cubes

- 1 pound Brussels sprouts, trimmed and sliced in half

- 1 small onion, diced

- 4 large eggs

Directions:

1. Preheat your oven to 425°F (220°C).

2. In a large bowl, toss the sweet potatoes,
    Brussels sprouts, onion, garlic, olive oil,
    smoked paprika, salt, and pepper together
    until everything is well coated.

3. Spread the vegetable mixture in a single layer
    on a baking sheet and roast for 20-25
    minutes, or until the sweet potatoes are
    tender and the Brussels sprouts are
    caramelized.

4. While the vegetables are roasting, fry the eggs
    in a non-stick skillet over medium heat to your
    desired level of d2ness.

5. Serve the roasted vegetables with the fried
    eggs on top.

VEGGIE MUSHROOM BURGERS

INGREDIENTS:

- 1/4 teaspoon red pepper flakes

- 1/2 teaspoon Italian seasoning

- 1/4 teaspoon onion powder

- 1/4 teaspoon garlic powder

- 1/2 teaspoon ginger powder

- 3/4 cup almond flour

- 1 egg

- 1 teaspoon chia seeds

- 1/4 teaspoon sea salt, more to taste

- 1/4 teaspoon black pepper, more to taste

- 1 teaspoon olive oil

- 16 ounces mushrooms, cut into 1/4 inch slices

- 1 red onion caramelized, cut into 1/4 inch slices

- 1 sweet potato, sliced thinly

- 1/4 cup walnuts, lightly toasted

Toppings:

- Tomato, sliced 1/4 inch thick

- Red onion, sliced thinly

- Pickles

- Mustard

- Ketchup

Directions:

1. Pre-heat oven to 400 °F.

2. In a medium skillet over high heat, cook mushrooms and onions until caramelized. About 8-10 minutes.

3. Place sweet potato on a sheet-tray lined with parchment paper. Toss in a teaspoon of olive oil, 2 teaspoon sea salt, and one teaspoon pepper. Roast for 15-20 minutes, or until fork tender.

4. In a food processor add mushrooms, onions, 1 cup of the cooked sweet potato, walnuts, spices, almond flour, egg and chia seeds. Pulse a few times until just combined, make sure not to over process the mixture. There should be pea like sized bits of sweet potato.

5. Line a sheet tray with parchment paper and bring the oven temperature down to 350 °F.

6. Shape the sweet potato and mushroom mixture into 6 one-inch patties.

7. Bake for 30 minutes or until the patties are firm to touch. Let cool for 5 minutes and serve warm with toppings of choice!

CAULIFLOWER PALEO GNOCCHI

Ingredients:

Gnocchi

- 3/4 cup cassava flour

- 1/2 teaspoon sea salt optional

- 4 cups cauliflower minced

Sauce

- 2 tablespoons tapioca flour

- salt and pepper to taste

- 1 can full fat canned coconut milk

- 4 cups spinach

- 2 large garlic cloves

Directions:

1. Heat oven to 425F.

2. Steam cauliflower for about five minutes until soft.

3. Ring water out of cauliflower by putting it in a dish towel and squeezing the excess water out. The remaining cauliflower should measure out to about 1 1/2 cups.

4. In a food processor blend ingredients for gnocchi until smooth (you may have to add more or less cassava flour to get the dough to be kneadable).

5. Separate dough into four equal parts and roll out into 3/4" diameter tubes on a surface dusted lightly with cassava flour. Cut the tubes of dough into 1" pieces.

6. Bring a large pot of water to a boil and drop gnocchi in. Once they have risen to the surface, remove, and drizzle lightly with olive oil.

7. Place gnocchi on a baking tray lined with parchment paper and lightly drizzled with

olive oil. Bake on 425F for 20 minutes, then turn gnocchi over and bake for another 20 minutes until golden.

8. In a saucepan stir together ingredients for sauce (except spinach) and whisk continuously (or use a hand blender) until smooth and the sauce begins to thicken.

9. If you overcook it, it will become too thick and gooey from the flour. Stir continuously to avoid clumping. Then remove from heat, add spinach, wilt it, then stir in gnocchi.

PUMPKIN STEEL-CUT OATS

Ingredients:

- 1/2 cup canned pumpkin purée

- 1/4 cup pumpkin seeds (pipits)

- 2 tablespoons maple syrup

- cups water

- 1 cup steel-cut oats

- Pinch salt

Directions:

1. Whip and reduce the heat to low. Simmer until the oats are soft, 20 to 30 minutes, continuing to stir occasionally.

2. Stir in the pumpkin purée and continue cooking on low for 3 to 5 minutes longer. Add the pumpkin seeds and maple syrup and season with salt.

3. Divide the oatmeal into four single-serving containers. Let cool before sealing the lids.

BARLEY BREAKFAST BOWL

Ingredients:

- Large pinch salt

- 1.1/2 cups dried cranberries

- 3 cups sweetened vanilla plant-based milk

- 1.1/2 cups pearl barley

- 3.3/4 cups water

- 2 tablespoons slivered almonds (optional)

Directions:

1. Put the barley, water, and salt. Bring to a boil.

2. Divide the barley into 6 jars or single-serving storage containers.

3. Attached the 1/4 cup of dried cranberries to each. Pour 1/2 cup of plant-based milk into each.

4. Attached the 1 teaspoon of slivered almonds (if using) to each. Close the jars tightly with lids.

BAKED AVOCADO EGGS

Ingredients:

- 2 medium/ large sized avocados, halve or pitted

- 4 large whole eggs

- ¼ teaspoons fresh ground black pepper

Directions:

1. Preheat your oven to 425 degrees F
2. Scoop out some pulp from the avocado halves, leaving enough space to fit an egg
3. Line an 8 by an 8-inch baking pan with foil, place avocado halves in the pan to fit nicely in a single layer
4. Gently fold the foil around the outer edges of the avocados
5. Crack 1 egg into each avocado half, season them with pepper

6. Bake for about 12-15 minutes uncovered until you have your desired d2ness

7. Remove from oven and let them rest for 5 minutes

8. Serve and enjoy!

CHILLED UP CINNAMON SMOOTHIE

Ingredients:

- ½ teaspoon cinnamon

- ¼ teaspoon vanilla extract

- 1 tablespoon chia seeds

- 1 cup unsweetened almond milk

- 2 tablespoons vanilla protein powder

- 1 cup ice cubs

Directions:

1. Add listed Ingredients: to a blender
2. Blend until you have a smooth and creamy texture
3. Serve chilled and enjoy!

PANCETTA

Ingredients:

- ½ cup toasted coconut flakes

- ½ cup toasted almond slivers

- ¾ cup multicolored bell peppers, diced

- 1 cup of pancetta

- Non-stick cooking spray

Directions:

1. Sauté pancetta in skillet over medium-high heat 1-2 minutes.
2. Mix pancetta with toasted coconut flakes, almond slivers, and diced bell peppers.

ORIENTAL INSPIRED RICE NOODLES AND STEW MEAT

Ingredients:

- 2 cloves garlic, thinly sliced

- ½ cup matchstick carrots

- 1 fresh jalapeno peppers, diced

- 1 can organic diced tomatoes

- 1 onion, sliced

- 4 cups beef or vegetable broth

- 1 cup worth rice noodles

- 1 teaspoon sesame oil

- ¼ teaspoon chili oil or paste

- ½ teaspoon ginger paste

- 1 teaspoon sweet paprika

- 1-pound stew meat

- ½ teaspoon diced oregano

Directions:

1. Brown stew meat and drain.

2. In crock pot combine sesame oil, chili oil or paste, ginger paste, sweet paprika, browned stew meat, ginger, matchstick carrots, jalapeno peppers, organic diced tomatoes, diced onion, and broth.

3. Let cook 30 minutes and add rice noodles and diced oregano.

SPROUTED BUCKWHEAT MUESLI

Ingredients:

- 20 g raw pumpkin seeds

- 20 g shelled raw sunflower seeds 80 gun sweetened shredded coconut

- 2 crisp, tart apples, grated down to the cores

  2 teaspoons ground cinnamon

- 1 litre unsweetened nut milk

- 330 g buckwheat groats 100 g raw pecans

- 50 g raw walnuts

- 4 tablespoons maple syrup (optional)

Directions:

1. Put the buckwheat groats in a bowl and cover
   with 1 litre filtered water. Set aside to soak for
   2 hours at room temperature.

2. Drain the buckwheat in a colander and rinse
   well. Transfer to a shallow container, cover
   with a clean tea towel and leave to sit at room
   temperature until the grouts begin to sprout,
   at least 8 hours or even overnight. Rinse and
   drain well.

3. While the buckwheat soaks, combine all the
   nuts and seeds in a bowl. Cover with about 5

cm of filtered water and set aside to soak at room temperature for 2 to 4 hours. Drain and rinse.

4. Put the sprouted buckwheat in a large bowl, add the soaked nuts and seeds, the coconut, grated apples and cinnamon and stir to combine.

5. Divide the muesli between 4 serving bowls and pour in 250 ml of the nut milk. Drizzle 1 tablespoon maple syrup, if using, over each portion and serve.

PEGAN PANCAKES

Ingredients:

- 2 medium bananas

- 3-4 packets stevia

- 1 tsp baking soda

- 1 1/2 cups almond flour

- 4 large eggs

- 1/2 cup water

Directions:

1. Put all the Ingredients: into the blender.
2. Blend for 15-20 minutes, until smooth (don't over blend or it will get warm).
3. Pour into a bowl.
4. Heat a griddle or heavy saute pan on medium-low heat. Lightly brush with butter or ghee.

5. Add batter in small circles - about 1 tablespoon per pancake.

6. When the edges start to look dry and the pancake is firm enough to flip (about 3 minutes), flip and cook another minute or 3 on the other side.

7. Place onto a plate and cover to keep warm. Repeat with the rest of the batter.

8. Serve with berries.

COLLARD GREEN OMELET

Ingredients:

- 3 tbsp unsalted butter, separated into individual tablespoons

- 1 lb baby hearty greens (beet greens, collard greens, dandelion greens, or mustard greens), remove stems if needed

- 4 large eggs

- ½-inch piece American pancetta or 4 oz bacon, diced

- ¼ cup vegetable stock, or chicken stock, water

- Chopped fresh parsley

- A few drops of chipotle hot sauce, or favored hot sauce

- Dash of chardonnay vinegar

- A pinch of salt

- A pinch of black pepper, ground

Directions:

1. In 2 pan, melt a tablespoon of butter over medium heat.
2. Add the pancetta or bacon and cook for about 10 minutes or until crispy.
3. Add the greens of choice with stock or water, vinegar, and hot sauce.
4. Cook the greens in this mixture for about five minutes or until just wilted.
5. Add more of the stock or water if the greens dry out before they have softened.
6. Season with salt and pepper.
7. In a second pan, add 2 tablespoons of butter and heat until it starts to simmer.
8. Beat the eggs until they are fluffy then sprinkle with salt and pepper.

9. Add the egg mixture into the pan and cook for about a minute until the bottom is just setting.

10. Raise the edge of the cooked egg and allow the liquid egg to flow in under.

11. Repeat with all edges of the cooked egg until there is no more liquid egg remaining.

12. Add the cooked greens to the center of the omelet and roll it into the shape of a cylinder.

13. Add the omelet to a plate and season with salt and pepper, topped with parsley.

SWEET POTATO TOAST WITH EGG AND AVOCADO

Ingredients:

- 1 tsp extra virgin olive oil

- ¼ cup sunflower sprouts or pea shoots

- A pinch of salt and pepper, for taste

- 2 sweet potato slices, washed well

- 2 eggs

- ½ avocado, sliced

- 1 tbsp butter

Directions:

1. Create 3 slices of sweet potato cut lengthwise. These slices should be ¼-inch thick.

2. In a toaster cook these slices for about 5 minutes a side.

3. While the sweet potato is toasting, cook the 3
   eggs.

4. In a pan melt the butter over medium-high
   heat and coat the whole pan.

5. Crack the eggs into the pan, cook to the
   desired thoroughness and flip over if you
   wish.

6. Remove eggs from the heat.

7. When the sweet potatoes are fully toasted
   add the avocado slices before adding the eggs
   on top.

8. Season with salt and pepper, a drizzle of olive
   oil, and sprouts or shoots of choice.

BUTTERNUT SQUASH SOUP

Ingredients:

- ½ teaspoon ground cinnamon

- ¼ teaspoon ground nutmeg

- ¼ teaspoon cayenne pepper

- Salt and pepper to taste

- 1 medium peeled, seeded, and cubed butternut squash

- 1 onion, chopped

- 2 garlic cloves, minced

- 4 cups vegetable broth

- Fresh parsley for garnish

Directions:

1. In a large pot, sauté the chopped onion and minced garlic until translucent.

2. Add the cubed butternut squash, vegetable broth, cinnamon, nutmeg, cayenne pepper (if using), salt, and pepper.

3. Bring the mixture to a boil, then reduce to a low heat and continue to cook for 20 to 25 minutes, or until the squash is soft.

4. Puree the contents with an immersion blender or in a blender until smooth.

5. Adjust the seasoning if needed. Serve hot, garnished with fresh parsley.

LENTIL AND VEGETABLE STEW

Ingredients:

- 2 garlic cloves, minced

- 1 can diced tomatoes

- 4 cups vegetable broth

- 1 teaspoon ground cumin

- 1 teaspoon smoked paprika

- ½ teaspoon dried thyme

- 1 cup washed and drained dried green lentils

- 1 onion, chopped

- 2 carrots, diced

- 2 celery stalks, diced

- Salt and pepper to taste

- Fresh cilantro for garnish

Directions:

1. Cook the chopped onion, carrots, celery, and minced garlic in a large pot until softened.

2. Add the rinsed lentils, diced tomatoes, vegetable broth, cumin, smoked paprika, dried thyme, salt, and pepper.

3. Bring the mixture to a boil, then reduce to a low heat and continue to cook for 25-30 minutes, or until the lentils are cooked.

4. Adjust the seasoning if needed. Serve hot, garnished with fresh cilantro.

QUINOA SALAD

Ingredients:

- ¼ cup sliced and pitted Klamath olives

- 2 tablespoons chopped fresh parsley

- 2 tablespoons chopped fresh mint

- Juice of 1 lemon

- 2 tablespoons extra virgin olive oil

- 1 cup cooked quinoa

- 1 cucumber, diced

- 1 red bell pepper, diced

- ½ cup cherry tomatoes, halved

- Salt and pepper to taste

Directions:

1. In a large bowl, combine cooked quinoa, diced cucumber, diced red bell pepper, cherry tomatoes, Klamath olives, parsley, and mint.

2. In a small bowl, whisk together the lemon juice, extra virgin olive oil, salt, and pepper.

3. Pour the dressing over the salad and toss to combine.

4. Adjust the seasoning if needed. Serve chilled

SWEET POTATO AND BLACK BEAN ENCHILADAS

Ingredients:

- 2 teaspoon of ground cumin

- 2 teaspoon of chilli powder

- 1/2 teaspoon smoked paprika

- Salt and pepper to taste

- 2 can (15 ounces) of enchilada sauce

- Eight small flour tortillas

- 1 cup shredded cheese (cheddar or Mexican blend)

- 3 large sweet potatoes, peeled and diced

- 2 can (15 ounces) of black beans, rinsed and drained

- 2 small onion, finely chopped

- 3 cloves garlic, minced

- 2 tablespoon of olive oil

- Chopped fresh cilantro for garnish (optional)

- Sour cream for serving (optional)

Directions:

1. Preheat your oven to 375°F (190°C).

2. heat the olive oil over medium heat in a large skillet. Add the onion and garlic, and sauté until the onion is translucent and fragrant, about 2-3 minutes.

3. Add the diced sweet potatoes to the skillet and cook for about 10 minutes, stirring occasionally, until tender.

4. Add the black beans, cumin, chilli powder, smoked paprika, salt, and pepper to the skillet. Stir well to combine all the Ingredients: and cook for an additional 2-3 minutes.

5. Pour about 1/3 cup of enchilada sauce into the bottom of a baking dish.

6. Place a tortilla on a clean surface and spoon about 1/4 cup of the sweet potato and black bean mixture onto the centre of the tortilla. Roll it up tightly and place it seam-side down in the baking dish.

7. Repeat this process with the remaining tortillas and filling.

8. Pour the remaining enchilada sauce over the rolled tortillas, ensuring they are all coated. Sprinkle the shredded cheese evenly over the top.

9. Cover the baking dish with foil and bake in the preheated oven for 25 minutes. Then, remove the foil and bake for 10-15 minutes until the cheese is bubbly and lightly browned.

10. Once cooked, remove the enchiladas from the oven and let them cool for a few minutes. Garnish with chopped cilantro, if desired.

11. Serve the Sweet Potato and Black Bean
Enchiladas warm, with a dollop of sour cream
on top if you like. Enjoy!

MUSHROOM AND SPINACH STUFFED PORTOBELLO MUSHROOMS

Ingredients:

- 1 cup mushrooms, finely chopped

- 1/2 cup breadcrumbs

- 1/2 cup grated Parmesan cheese

- 1/2 teaspoon dried thyme

- Four large Portobello mushrooms

- 2 tablespoons olive oil

- 3 cloves garlic, minced

- 2 small onion, finely chopped

- 2 cups baby spinach, chopped

- Salt and pepper to taste

Directions:

1. Preheat the oven to 375°F (190°C). Clean the Portobello mushrooms and remove the stems. Place them on a baking sheet, gill side up.

2. In a skillet, heat the olive oil over medium heat. Add the garlic and onion, and sauté until softened and fragrant, about 3 minutes.

3. Add the baby spinach and chopped mushrooms to the skillet. Cook until the spinach wilts and the mushrooms release their moisture, about 5 minutes. Remove from heat.

4. In a bowl, combine the cooked spinach and mushrooms with breadcrumbs, Parmesan cheese, dried thyme, salt, and pepper. Stir well to combine.

5. Divide the stuffing mixture evenly among the Portobello mushrooms, filling the caps generously.

6. Bake the stuffed mushrooms in the preheated oven for about 20 minutes or until the mushrooms are tender and the stuffing is golden brown.

7. Once cooked, remove from the oven and let them cool slightly before serving.

VEGAN QUINOA & BLACK BEAN STUFFED PEPPERS

Ingredients:

- 1 small diced onion,

- 1 diced red pepper,

- 2 cloves of minced garlic,

- 1 tsp cumin powder,

- 1 tsp chili powder,

- 4 bell peppers

- 1 cup of cooked quinoa

- 1 can of black beans

- Salt and pepper to taste

Directions:

1. Preheat the oven to 375 F. Cut the tops off
   the bell peppers and remove the seeds and
   membranes.

2. In a skillet over medium heat, sauté the onion,
   red pepper and garlic until softened.

3. Add the cumin and chili powder and cook for
   a minute more. Stir in the quinoa, black
   beans, and some salt and pepper.

4. Stuff the pepper halves with the quinoa
   mixture and place them on a baking sheet.
   Bake for 25-30 minutes, or until the peppers
   are tender.

AVOCADO & TOMATO SALAD

Ingredients:

- 1/4 cup chopped cilantro,

- 1/4 cup diced red onion,

- 2 tbsp lime juice,

- 2 ripe avocados,

- 2 tomatoes,

- Salt and pepper to taste

Directions:

1. Cut the avocados and tomatoes into small pieces. In a large mixing bowl, combine the avocado, tomatoes, cilantro, red onion, lime juice, and some salt and pepper.

2. Toss gently until well mixed. Serve chilled.

COCONUT FLOUR BANANA BREAD

Ingredients:

- 1/4 cup maple syrup or h2y

- 1 teaspoon vanilla extract

- 1/2 cup coconut flour

- 1 teaspoon baking powder

- 1/2 teaspoon cinnamon

- 4 ripe bananas, mashed

- 4 large eggs

- 1/4 cup coconut oil, melted

- Pinch of salt

- Optional add-ins: chopped nuts, dark chocolate chips, dried fruit

Directions:

1. Preheat the oven to 350°F (175°C) and grease
    a loaf pan.
2. In a large bowl, whisk together the mashed
    bananas, eggs, melted coconut oil, maple
    syrup (or h2y), and vanilla extract.
3. In a separate bowl, combine the coconut
    flour, baking powder, cinnamon, and salt.
4. Add the dry Ingredients: to the wet
    Ingredients: and stir until well combined.
5. If desired, fold in chopped nuts, dark
    chocolate chips, or dried fruit.
6. Pour the batter into the greased loaf pan and
    smooth the top with a spatula.
7. Bake for 45-55 minutes, or until a toothpick
    inserted into the center of the bread comes
    out clean.
8. Remove the banana bread from the oven and
    let it cool in the pan for 10 minutes.
9. Transfer the bread to a wire rack to cool
    completely before slicing.

MIXED BERRY CRUMBLE

Ingredients:

For the filling

- 1 tablespoon lemon juice

- 1 tablespoon tapioca flour or cornstarch

- 4 cups mixed berries (strawberries, blueberries, raspberries)

- 2 tablespoons maple syrup or h2y

For the crumble topping

- 2 tablespoons coconut oil, melted

- 2 tablespoons maple syrup or h2y

- 1 teaspoon vanilla extract

- 1 cup almond flour

- 1/4 cup coconut flour

- 1/4 cup chopped almonds or walnuts

- Pinch of salt

Directions:

1. Preheat the oven to 350°F (175°C) and lightly grease a baking dish.

2. In a bowl, combine the mixed berries, maple syrup (or h2y), lemon juice, and tapioca flour (or cornstarch). Toss to coat the berries evenly.

3. Transfer the berry mixture to the greased baking dish.

4. In a separate bowl, combine the almond flour, coconut flour, chopped almonds (or walnuts), melted coconut oil, maple syrup (or h2y), vanilla extract, and salt. Mix until crumbly.

5. Sprinkle the crumble topping evenly over the berry mixture in the baking dish.

6. Bake for 25-30 minutes, or until the topping is golden brown and the berry filling is bubbling.

7. Remove from the oven and let it cool for a

  few minutes before serving.

<h1 style="text-align:center">COCONUT CHIA PUDDING:</h1>

Ingredients:

- 1 cup coconut milk

- 1 tablespoon pure maple syrup or h2y

- 1/2 teaspoon vanilla extract

- 1/4 cup chia seeds

- Fresh berries and shredded coconut for topping

Directions:

1. Combine the chia seeds, maple syrup, coconut milk, and vanilla extract in a bowl. Mix well to guarantee the chia seeds are equitably appropriated.

2. Cover the bowl and refrigerate the combination for no less than 2 hours or

expedite to permit the chia seeds to retain the fluid and make a pudding-like consistency.

3. Prior to serving, mix the pudding to ensure there are no protuberances. On the off chance that the pudding is excessively thick, you can add a sprinkle of coconut milk to arrive at your ideal consistency.

4. Top the chia pudding with new berries and destroyed coconut for added flavor and surface.

5. To start your day on a healthy and delicious note, make these Paleo breakfast recipes, which are simple to prepare and packed with nutritious Ingredients:. Take pleasure in your nutritious and filling Paleo breakfast!

GRILLED PALEO CHICKEN SALAD

Ingredients:

- 1/2 red chime pepper, hacked

- 1/4 red onion, daintily cut

- 1/4 cup cherry tomatoes, split

- 2 tablespoons extra-virgin olive oil

- 1 tablespoon balsamic vinegar

- 2 b2less, skinless chicken bosoms

- 2 cups blended salad greens

- 1/2 cucumber, cut

- Salt and pepper to taste

Directions:

1. Preheat the barbecue to medium-high intensity.

2. Season the chicken bosoms with salt and pepper.

3. Barbecue the chicken for around 4-5 minutes for every side, or until cooked through and at this point not pink in the middle.

4. Eliminate the chicken from the barbecue and let it rest for a couple of moments prior to cutting it into slight strips.

5. In a huge bowl, prepare together the plate of mixed greens, cucumber, red chime pepper, red onion, and cherry tomatoes.

6. Toss the salad with the balsamic vinegar and olive oil to coat the Ingredients:.

7. Top the serving of mixed greens with the cut barbecued chicken and season with extra salt and pepper whenever wanted.

AVOCADO PESTO AND PALEO ZUCCHINI NOODLES

Ingredients:

- 1/4 cup pine nuts

- 2 cloves garlic

- Juice of 1 lemon

- 3 tablespoons extra-virgin olive oil

- Salt and pepper to taste

- 2 medium zucchinis, spiral zed into noodles

- 1 ready avocado, hollowed and stripped

- 1 cup new basil leaves

- Discretionary fixings: cherry tomatoes, cut dark olives, ground Parmesan (if not severe Paleo)

Directions:

1. In a food processor, consolidate the avocado, basil, pine nuts, garlic, lemon juice, and olive oil. Mix until you have a smooth and velvety pesto sauce.

2. In an enormous skillet, heat a tablespoon of olive oil over medium intensity.

3. The zucchini noodles should be sautéed in the skillet for 3 to 4 minutes, or until they are soft but still a little bit firm.

4. Eliminate the skillet from the intensity and throw the zucchini noodles with the avocado pesto until they are uniformly covered.

5. Season with salt and pepper to taste.

6. Serve the zucchini noodles with discretionary fixings like cherry tomatoes, cut dark olives, or ground Parmesan for added flavor and surface.

SUPER GREEN SMOOTHIE

Ingredients:

- 1 tsp. wheatgrass

- 1 c. kale

- ½ c. organic orange juice

- ½ c. ice

- 4 c. spinach

Directions:

1. Steam kale and spinach and set aside to cool.

2. Put the Ingredients:in a blender and mix until smooth.

3. Serve and enjoy.

SUPERFOOD SMOOTHIE

Ingredients:

- 1 peeled and chopped frozen banana

- 1½ c. chilled unsweetened almond milk

- 1 c. trimmed and chopped fresh kale

- 2 tsps. chia seeds

- 1 tbsp. matcha green tea powder

- 1 cup chopped fresh baby spinach

- ½ c. frozen pineapple chunks

Directions:

1. In a high-speed blender, pulse all the Ingredients:until smooth.
2. Put into 2 large serving glasses and serve immediately.

ASPARAGUS SOUP

Ingredients:

- ¼ lb. asparagus trimmed and cut

- ½ tsp. fennel

- ½ tsp. thyme

- ½ tsp. dill

- 1 c. vegetable stock

- ½ c. water

- ½ c. leeks chopped

- salt and pepper to taste

Directions:

1. Begin by sauteing the asparagus and fennel for five minutes in a pan set over medium-high heat.

2. Then add in the vegetable stock and water
    and allow the soup to come to boil.

3. When the mixture reaches a boil, reduce the
    heat and allow to simmer for 10-12 minutes.

4. After the soup has simmered, add in the herbs
    and use an immersion blender to blend the
    vegetables until smooth.

5. Season with salt and pepper before serving.
    Enjoy!

DETOX SALAD

INGREDIENTS:

- Orange peel, seeded and diced into small pieces

- 6 tablespoons extra virgin olive oil

- 4 tablespoons lime juice only use freshly squeezed, not the kind in a bottle

- 2 tablespoon almond butter

- 3 tablespoons honey optional

- 1 inch ginger peeled and finely grated. *only use fresh ginger, not powder

- 4 cups red cabbage very thinly sliced and loosely packed in the cup

- 4 cups kale thinly sliced kale, no stems and loosely packed in the cup

- 1/4 cup cilantro chopped into small pieces, loosely packed. *hint i like to bunch my cilantro all together and cut with scissors

- 1 cup yellow pepper diced into small pieces note: you could also add red, orange, and green peppers too if you prefer.

- ½ cup pumpkin seeds

- 1/2 cup pomegranate seeds

- 1 cup green apple one medium thinly sliced

- ½ teaspoon salt

Directions:

Salad dressing

1. In a small jar that has a lid, mix together the olive oil, lime juice, almond butter, grated ginger, honey, and salt. Shake until smooth and blended well.

Salad

2. Toss cabbage, kale, cilantro, apples, pumpkin seeds, yellow pepper, oranges, and pomegranate seeds in a medium-sized bowl.
3. Drizzle the salad dressing over the veggies, stirring until the salad dressing is evenly distributed throughout the salad.

RAINBOW SALAD WITH CITRUS DRESSING

Ingredients:

For the salad:

- 1 small red onion, thinly sliced

- 1 cup cherry tomatoes, halved

- 1\/2 cup shredded purple cabbage

- 1/4 cup fresh cilantro leaves

- 1/4 cup fresh mint leaves

- 1/4 cup sliced almonds (optional, for garnish)

- 1 cup baby spinach leaves

- 1 cup mixed salad greens

- 1 small red bell pepper, thinly sliced

- 1 small yellow bell pepper, thinly sliced

- 1 small orange bell pepper, thinly sliced

- 1 small cucumber, thinly sliced

- 1 medium carrot, julienned

For the citrus dressing:

- Juice of 1 lime

- 2 tablespoons extra virgin olive oil

- 1 tablespoon h2y or maple syrup (optional, for sweetness)

- Juice of 1 orange

- Juice of 1 lemon

- Salt and pepper to taste

Directions:

1. In a large salad bowl, combine the baby spinach, mixed salad greens, and all the sliced and julienned vegetables, including bell

peppers, cucumber, carrot, red onion, cherry tomatoes, and purple cabbage.

2. Toss the salad lightly to mix all of the substances.

3. In a separate small bowl, whisk together the orange juice, lemon juice, lime juice, extra virgin olive oil, h2y or maple syrup (if using), salt, and pepper.

4. Adjust the sweetness and seasoning according to your taste preferences.

5. Pour the citrus dressing over the salad and toss well to ensure all the vegetables are evenly coated.

6. Add the fresh cilantro and mint leaves to the salad and gently toss again.

7. Sprinkle the sliced almonds on top for an extra crunchy and nutty flavor, if desired.

8. Serve the Rainbow Salad with Citrus Dressing immediately and enjoy the burst of flavors and vibrant colors.

9. This salad is not only a feast for the eyes but also a great way to incorporate a wide range of vegetables into your diet.

10. The citrus dressing adds a tangy and refreshing element that perfectly complements the crispness of the vegetables.

11. Feel free to customize the salad by adding or substituting Ingredients: based on your preference and seasonal availability.

QUINOA PORRIDGE WITH ALMONDS, CHIA, AND COCONUT

Ingredients:

- 1/4 cup shredded coconut

- 1/4 cup sliced almonds

- 1 tablespoon chia seeds

- 1/2 teaspoon ground cinnamon

- 1 cup quinoa, rinsed

- 2 cups water

- 1 cup unsweetened almond milk

- 1/4 teaspoon salt

- Optional: h2y or maple syrup for sweetness

Directions:

1. In a medium saucepan, bring the quinoa and water to a boil. Reduce the heat to low and let it simmer, covered, for 15-20 minutes or until the water is absorbed and the quinoa is tender.

2. Stir in the almond milk, shredded coconut, sliced almonds, chia seeds, cinnamon, and salt.

3. Cook the mixture over medium heat, stirring occasionally, for 5-7 minutes or until the mixture has thickened to a porridge consistency.

4. Taste and add h2y or maple syrup if desired.

5. Serve hot, garnished with additional sliced almonds, shredded coconut, and cinnamon if desired.

CHIA SEED PUDDING WITH COCONUT MILK AND BERRIES

Ingredients:

- 1-2 tablespoons h2y or maple syrup (optional)

- 1/2 teaspoon vanilla extract

- 1/2 cup chia seeds

- 1 can (13.5 oz) coconut milk

- 1 cup mixed berries (fresh or frozen)

Directions:

1. In a large bowl, whisk together the chia seeds, coconut milk, h2y or maple syrup (if using), and vanilla extract until well combined.
2. Let the mixture sit for about 5 minutes to thicken.
3. Whisk again to ensure that there are no clumps of chia seeds.
4. Cover the bowl and refrigerate for at least 2 hours, or overnight.

5. Before serving, give the pudding a good stir to make sure that it is evenly mixed.

6. Spoon the pudding into individual serving dishes and top with the mixed berries.

2-PAN EGGS WITH ASPARAGUS AND TOMATOES

Ingredients:

- 1 pint cherry tomatoes

- 4 eggs

- 2 tablespoons olive oil

- 2 teaspoons chopped fresh thyme

- 2 pounds asparagus

- Salt and pepper to taste

Directions:

1. Preheat the oven to 400°F. Grease a baking sheet with non-stick cooking spray.

2. Arrange the asparagus and cherry tomatoes in an even layer on the baking sheet. Drizzle the olive oil over the vegetables; season with the thyme and salt and pepper to taste.

3. Roast in the oven until the asparagus is nearly tender and the tomatoes are wrinkled, 10 to 12 minutes.

4. Crack the eggs on top of the asparagus; season each with salt and pepper.

5. Return to the oven and bake until the egg whites are set, but the yolks are still jiggly, 7-8 minutes more.

6. To serve, divide the asparagus, tomatoes and eggs among four plates.

CASHEW CRUNCH SALAD WITH SESAME DRESSING

Ingredients:

For the Salad:

- 1–2 cup roasted cashews (see notes)

- 2 cups crunchy chow mein noodles (optional)

- chicken, shrimp, or any other protein you like

- 1/2 head of green cabbage, finely shredded

- 1/2 head of purple cabbage, finely shredded

- 2 cups carrots, matchstick-cut or shredded

- 1 cup fresh cilantro, chopped

- 1/2 cup sliced green onion

- 2 cups cooked edamame (see notes)

Dressing:

- 2 tablespoons sugar

- 1 teaspoon salt

- a few shakes of garlic powder

- 1/4 cup olive oil (you can use any other oil as well)

- 3 tablespoons white vinegar

- 2 tablespoons sesame oil – very important for flavor!

- optional: 1/4 cup Greek yogurt or mayo (more or less to taste)

Directions:

1. Shake the dressing Ingredients: up in a jar until smooth.
2. Add the Greek yogurt or mayo (optional just makes it more creamy) and shake again until smooth. YUM.

3. Toss all the salad Ingredients: together.

    Drizzle with dressing and serve!

QUINOA BREAKFAST PORRIDGE

Ingredients:

- 1/2 tsp. vanilla

- 1/2 tsp. cinnamon

- 1 cup dry quinoa

- 2 cups almond milk

- 1 tbsp. agave or maple syrup

- 1 tablespoon ground flax meal

Directions:

1. Combine quinoa, almond milk, sugar, vanilla, and cinnamon in a little pot. Heat to the point of boiling and lessen to a stew.

2. Allow the quinoa to cook until the majority of the fluid is retained and quinoa is fleecy (15-20 minutes). Blend in the flax meal. Blend in

any extra toppers or include INS, and

appreciate.

GRAPES AND GREEN TEA SMOOTHIE

Ingredients:

- 1 banana, peeled

- 1-inch piece of ginger

- ½ cup of ice cubes

- 2 cups baby spinach

- ½ cup green tea

- ½ cup of green grapes

- ½ of a medium apple, peeled, diced

Directions:

1. In the container of a high-speed food processor or blender, combine all of the Ingredients: in the order specified in the Ingredients: list and then cover with the lid.

2. Pulse for 1 minute until smooth, and then
    serve.

CHIA AND FLAX PORRIDGE

Ingredients:

- 1 tablespoon ground flaxseed

- 1/3 cup coconut cream

- ½ cup of water

- 1 teaspoon vanilla extract

- 1 tablespoon chia seeds

- 1 tablespoon butter

Directions:

1. Add chia seeds, coconut cream, flaxseed, water, and vanilla to a small pot

2. Stir and let it sit for 5 minutes

3. Add butter and place pot over low heat

4. Keep stirring as butter melts

5. Once the porridge is hot/not boiling, pour it into a bowl

6. Enjoy!

7. Add a few berries or a dash of cream for extra

flavour

MORNING FLAVORFUL HASH

Ingredients:

- ½ teaspoon paprika

- 1 tablespoon olive oil

- 1 cup Brussels sprouts, halved

- ¼ onion, diced

- 1 tablespoon parsley

- ¼ cup red bell pepper, diced

- ½ teaspoon black pepper

- ½ teaspoon salt

- ½ teaspoon garlic powder

- 1 large turnip, peeled and diced

Directions:

1. Take a large-sized skillet and place it over medium-high heat

2. Add turnips and season with spices, cook for about 5-7 minutes, making sure to stir in from time to time

3. Add onion, Brussels, and cook for 3 minutes more until tender

4. Add red bell pepper and cook for 5 minutes more

5. Garnish with a bit of parsley, and serve

6. Enjoy!

FRIENDLY STEAK AND SHRIMP

Ingredients:

- 1 teaspoon paprika

- ½ teaspoon pepper

- 2 diced scallions

- 1 teaspoon Worcestershire sauce

- ½ teaspoon chili powder

- 1 teaspoon diced parsley

- 1/3 cup sliced mushrooms

- 2 3 - oz. sirloin steaks

- 8 medium shrimp

- 2 tablespoon butter or ghee

- 2/3 tablespoon white wine

- 1/3 teaspoon chicken granules

- ¼ cup pine nuts (optional)

Directions:

1. In a plastic bag combine shrimp, butter or ghee, white wine, chicken granules, parsley, paprika, pepper. Marinate in fridge 30 minutes.

2. Mix together Worcestershire sauce, chili powder, parsley, sliced mushrooms, then cook steak 4-5 minutes per side.

3. Transfer d2 steaks to a plate and top with mushroom mix and pine nuts. Cook shrimp 1-2 minutes, transfer to plate, and serve.

PROTEIN STIR FRY

Ingredients:

- 4 plum tomatoes, sliced into wedges

- 2 scallions, thinly sliced

- 1 teaspoon turmeric

- Coconut or avocado oil

- 6-7 eggs, beaten

- Favorite herbs

Directions:

1. Scramble eggs and stir in sliced tomatoes, sliced scallions, turmeric and diced herbs.